THE RACHMANINOFF PIANO ANTHOLOGY
27 PIECES FOR SOLO PIANO

This edition includes editorial commentary and musical texts from the following editions published by
Boosey & Hawkes Music Publishers Ltd:

Serge Rachmaninoff	*Preludes for Piano*	(HL48010804; ISMN M-060-06593-4)
Serge Rachmaninoff	*Etudes-Tableaux*	(HL48010858; ISMN M-060-07121-8)
Serge Rachmaninoff	*Piano Compositions, Vol. 1*	(HL48018951; ISMN M-060-11649-0)
Serge Rachmaninoff	*Piano Compositions, Vol. 3*	(HL48012261; ISMN M-060-11572-1)

ISBN 978-1-4803-8677-8

DISTRIBUTED BY

HAL•LEONARD®
CORPORATION

7777 W. BLUEMOUND RD. P.O. BOX 13819 MILWAUKEE, WI 53213

www.boosey.com
www.halleonard.com

CONTENTS

SERGE RACHMANINOFF
(1873-1943)

Serge Rachmaninoff was born in Oneg in the government of Novgorod in 1873, and died in Los Angeles in 1943. As a student at the St. Petersburg and Moscow Conservatories he was always a naturally brilliant pianist — his piano professors included Alexander Siloti and Nikolai Zverev — but he was always more inclined towards composition, studying with Arensky and Taneiev.

At this early age his style was already remarkably original, as exemplified by the set of piano pieces Op. 3 — the second of which is the famous prelude in C-sharp minor — and the opera *Aleko*, with which he won the Great Gold Medal of the Moscow Conservatoire in 1892. Until the disastrous premiere of his first symphony at the age of 24, music flowed profusely from his pen.

Rachmaninoff's confidence took such a blow as a result of the wretched performance and scathing reviews which the First Symphony received, that he was unable to compose again for three years. His famous recovery under treatment by the hypnotist Dr. Nikolai Dahl resulted in a profusion of fresh and inspired works, including his Suite No. 2 for two pianos Op. 17, the Second Piano Concerto Op. 18, the Cello Sonata Op. 19, the Variations on a Theme of Chopin Op. 22, and the Ten Preludes for Piano Op. 23. These pieces have all the hallmarks of Rachmaninoff's more popular style, with an abundance of memorable melodies and his own combination of disarming, deceptively simple harmonies and complex chromaticism. Together these produce a uniquely nostalgic effect, totally Russian in inspiration, and reveling in the increasing capacity of the piano as a sonorous instrument, something which the composer was admirably equipped to do.

It is instructive, when considering the interpretation of Rachmaninoff's piano works, to remember the primary qualities of his own playing. He was known as the 'Puritan Pianist' for his close adherence to the printed note and indications, faithful and uneccentric rhythms, unsentimental ideas and mastery of musical architecture.

It seems to the present writer that Rachmaninoff's notation of dynamics and phrasing, and in particular his carefully worked out tempo indications and relationships, are a quite sufficient guide to the interpretation of this music. Care should be taken not to distort these, also to resist the urge to sentimentalize.

— Peter Donohoe

PUBLISHER'S NOTE: MORCEAUX DE FANTAISIE, OP. 3, & MORCEAUX DE SALON, OP. 10

Rachmaninoff's five *Morceaux de Fantaisie* were composed in 1892 and published as Op. 3 by A. Gutheil in Moscow the following year; the seven *Morceaux de Salon* composed in 1893/4 were published by the same firm in 1894 as Op. 10. Both sets were subsequently re-engraved by Breitkopf & Härtel in Leipzig and reissued by Gutheil. For the present publication in Boosey & Hawkes' Authentic Edition of the composer's works, the following sources have been used:

Op. 3, Nos. 1 & 2: masters from the Boosey & Hawkes archives; Nos. 3, 4 & 5: photographic copies of the re-engraved Gutheil editions in the British Library. Careful reference to photocopies of the original MSS, now in the Glinka Museum, Moscow, has enabled many details (especially dynamics) to be amended.

Op. 10, Nos. 17: a generally reliable early edition has been used as master text, after careful checking for errors and discrepancies. Reference to the re-engraved Russian Collected Edition Volume 1, published in 1948 under the general editorship of Pavel Lamm, has also been made where appropriate.

Thanks are extended to the following: The British Library for supplying photographs of Op. 3, Nos. 3, 4 & 5; Mr. Geoffrey Norris, for putting photocopies of the manuscripts of the five Op. 3 pieces at our disposal; Mr. Robert Threlfall, who has checked and coordinated all the available material and read proofs at each stage of the production.

London, 1996, 2003

PUBLISHER'S NOTE: MOMENTS MUSICAUX, OP. 16

The six *Moments musicaux*, Op. 16 were composed in October–December 1896 and were immediately engraved and published in Moscow by P. Jurgenson. Later, some re-engraved editions from other houses altered the composer's carefully considered phrasing and added inauthentic fingering and pedaling instructions (which Rachmaninoff had indicated only for No. 4). The present publication reproduces Jurgenson's original text but with the correction of the very few errors since noted in that edition.

Boosey & Hawkes offers grateful acknowledgement to Mr. Robert Threlfall for considerable assistance and advice given during the preparation of this publication.

January 2005

Music text checked by Robert Threlfall

PRELUDES, OP. 23, & OP. 32

Ten Preludes, Op. 23

The set of Preludes, Op. 23, begins in a gloomy mood, and seems to follow on from the final bars of Op. 3, No. 2, without any apparent gulf between the two different stages in the composer's output. The beautiful No. 4 is idyllic in mood, with a long singing melody accompanied typically by widely spaced arpeggios. The central climax anticipates very closely that of the intermezzo of the Third Piano Concerto.

No. 5 is orchestral in style, both in its bravura *alla marcia* outer sections, and in its lyrical and nostalgic central episode.

Returning to the same mood as No. 4, Prelude No. 6 has great beauty of shape, both in the melody and characteristic counter-melody, and also in the sixteenth-note accompaniment.

The ravishing final prelude of this set [Op. 23, No. 10] is also well-known in its arrangement for cello and piano, an entirely suitable instrumentation for its sentiment. A single, blissfully idyllic melody is expanded characteristically into a duo between the two hands, which also both share the accompaniment.

The Ten Preludes, Op. 23, were not published with the idea of ultimately completing a set of 24, following in the footsteps of Chopin, but the possibility soon occurred to the composer. A further thirteen preludes were published as Op. 32, following the Second Symphony, the First Piano Sonata, and the Third Piano Concerto.

Thirteen Preludes, Op. 32

The Op. 32 group is harmonically bolder in general than Op. 23, and in many ways the piano writing is even more original. Whereas Chopin looms to some extent above the earlier set, his spirit now seems more distant.

The rhythmically accompanied duet of No. 7 is calm, and seems to be a curious suspension of the mood of No. 6 before it returns with a vengeance in No. 8.

The great Prelude No. 10, is like a return to the mood of the early C-sharp minor Prelude, with its oppressive underlying feeling of tragedy and foreboding. It is known to have been inspired by Böcklin's painting 'The Return,' and again uses the bass notes of the piano to immensely sonorous effect.

By way of contrast the Prelude No. 11 is child-like and simple, based on a *siciliano* rhythm throughout.

— Peter Donohoe

Publisher's Note: Preludes, Op. 23, & Op. 32

Apart from two early piano pieces with the title Prelude, which were only published posthumously, Rachmaninoff's Prelude in C-sharp minor is the official first in his series; it is also one of the most famous piano compositions of its day. Written in 1892, it was published in 1893 by Edition A. Gutheil (no. 6516) as the second of a set of five *Morceaux de Fantaisie*, Op. 3.

Among the many compositions surrounding Rachmaninoff's Second Concerto is the set of Ten Preludes, Op. 23. The well-known fifth, in G minor, was written in 1901, the rest a couple of years later. Gutheil published them all, complete and in separate numbers, in 1903 (nos. 8338-47). Similarly, following the Third Concerto, comes the set of Thirteen Preludes, Op. 32. Composed in 1910, they were published at once by Gutheil, again complete and in separate numbers (nos. 9612-24).

Subsequently all 24 Preludes appeared in one book under the original publisher's imprint. Boosey & Hawkes Music Publishers Ltd. acknowledge the assistance of Mr. Robert Threlfall in checking the entire musical text against Xerox copies of the original manuscripts and (where available) proofs, in preparing the Editorial Report on the present reissue and in particular for the loan of a mint copy of an early Gutheil printing of the 24 Preludes from his own collection.

Editorial Report: Preludes, Op. 23, & Op. 32

The manuscripts of Rachmaninoff's 24
Preludes are to be found in the State Central
Glinka Museum of Musical Culture, Moscow,
Fond 18 (Op. 23) No. 8, folios 59-84; (Op. 32) No. 98.
Proofs, corrected by the composer, also survive in the
same collection, No. 95 (for Op. 23 Nos. 1-5 only)
and No. 99 (for Op. 32).

The first editions were published by A. Gutheil
in Moscow as follows:
Op. 23, in 1903, A8338-8347G
Op. 32, in 1910-11, A9612-9624G

Copies of all the above were available when
checking the printed text for the present
reprint, for which new masters were prepared by
photographing a mint copy of a later Gutheil
one-volume edition of the 24 Preludes.

Rachmaninoff prepared all his manuscripts for
publication with a characteristic precision which
renders any subsequent editorial work largely
redundant. There is hardly any ambiguity
concerning the notes, and his detailed
indications for performance were shown with
equal accuracy. He was likewise well served by
his engravers. Very few alterations appear in the
manuscripts; rewritings appear as follows:

Op. 32, No. 7:
bars 11-13 replace four original bars; bars 22-
25 likewise replace seven bars. In bars 34-37
the RH is rewritten and bars 44-45 replace six
deleted bars.

Op. 32, No. 10:
bar 48: three further bars in the manuscript,
there preceding the reprise after the cadenza,
have been deleted.

Of a few significant changes introduced by the
composer at the proof stage, the following
are the most interesting:

Op. 23, No. 4:
minor changes were made to the RH in bars 62
and 64 and to the LH in bars 47, 48, 49, and 77.

Op. 32, No. 11:
in bars 45-47 the *rit. … a tempo* was added at
the proof stage. The *ritenuto* over the last four
bars is not in the manuscript but had already
been engraved in the proofs now consulted.

Some minor errors in the original plates were
evidently overlooked by Rachmaninoff in his
proofreading. A very few omitted slurs, mostly
clear in the manuscripts, have now been
restored; various dots and dashes are likewise
silently replaced and a few misalignments in the
original engraving are now corrected.

Occasional missing accidentals may have been
"understood" by the composer, but are now
added, as are a few dynamics and directions
clear in the manuscripts.

Op. 23, No. 4:
in bar 21 the alignment of the melody is now
as in the manuscript. In bar 49 a D is added to
the third eighth-note chord in the RH, and in bar
60 a D is added to the third beat in the LH,
both as in the manuscript.

Op. 23, No. 6:
in bar 20 flat signs (not in the manuscript) are
added to the RH eighth-note octave C.

Op. 23, No. 10:
in bar 51, the RH eighth-note G at the half-bar
needs a flat sign (though not in the manuscript).

Op. 32, No. 7:
at bar 33 (*a tempo I*) is suggested, though not
in the manuscript.

Op. 32, No. 10:
in bars 3-4, 7-8, 9-10, 51-52, 55-56, and
57-58 it is clear from the manuscript that the
slurs refer to the lower voices and that the
upper half notes are not to be tied.

© Copyright 1992 by Robert Threlfall

ETUDES-TABLEAUX, OP. 33, & OP. 39

Rachmaninoff's recovery, under treatment by Dr. Dahl, from crippling depression and lack of confidence led to a profusion of inspired works between opus 17 and 30. It is this portion of his output, along with the much later Rhapsody on a Theme of Paganini, Op. 43, which has achieved the greatest popularity. This is undoubtedly because melodically the composer was at his most consistently memorable.

It is perhaps the inevitable musical snobbery with which this popularity tended to be greeted by the *cognoscenti*, combined with Rachmaninoff's personal insecurity that made him largely turn away from this style. From the Thirteen Preludes, Op. 32 onwards one notices a tendency to suppress overtly romantic melodies, to increase the floridness of accompanying passage-work, and to develop a progressively more brittle, abrasive and unpredictable harmonic language.

There are of course notable exceptions to this departure from the earlier style, for example the 18th Variation of the Rhapsody on a Theme of Paganini, the slow movement of the Third Symphony, and the central section of the Symphonic Dance No. 1, Op. 45, the main characteristic being the increasing sense of almost nostalgia and the underlying sadness of their great melodic lines. To some extent this can be attributed to the composer's emigration to the USA, which occurred immediately after the completion of the *Etudes-Tableaux*, Op. 39, and the love which he felt for his homeland. During his initial residence in America he was remarkedly non-productive. It was to be 15 years before he wrote his next – and final – piano solo work, the Variations on a Theme of Corelli, Op. 42.

It is against this background that we must view the *Etudes-Tableaux*. Those who look for heartfelt, romantic movements will probably be disappointed, except by Op. 39, No. 5, and it may be for this reason that they are seldom performed. This is regrettable, since they offer a wealth of musical invention and pianistic innovation, and, along with the Preludes, amount to a summation of, and testament to Rachmaninoff's unique piano style.

They are undoubtedly intended to be performed as two unified groups, but it is of course possible to make a representative selection from both sets, as with the preludes, or even to play certain ones singly. There is also a feeling of literary inspiration behind these works, which may explain the composer's choice of the title *Etudes-Tableaux*.

Etudes-Tableaux, Op. 33

In No. 3 the strange, somber but beautiful harmonies of the first section in C minor give way to the tranquility of the second section in departure from the tonic is during the wonderful passage of nine bars following the Poco a Poco Agitato, subsequently quoted at the end of the 2nd movement of the 4th Piano Concerto.

— Peter Donohoe

Publisher's Note: Etudes-Tableaux, Op. 33

The original edition of Op. 33, published in separate numbers by A. Gutheil, Leipzig, 1914, advertised nine pieces as follows:

No. 1 in F minor
No. 2 in C Major
No. 3 in C minor
No. 4 in A minor
No. 5 in D minor
No. 6 in E-flat minor
No. 7 in E-flat Major
No. 8 in G minor
No. 9 in C-sharp minor

Only six were actually issued at this time: Op. 33, No. 1 (A9686G), No. 2 (A9687G), No. 6 (A9691G), No. 7 (A9692G), No. 8 (A9693G), and No. 9 (A9694G). Later reprints by Gutheil (S. et N. Koussevitzky) suppress the previously advertised Nos. 3, 4, and 5.

No. 4 was withdrawn by Rachmaninoff from Op. 33, and subsequently (1920) published by Edition Russe de Musique as No. 6 of *Etudes-Tableaux*, Op. 39.

Nos. 3 and 5 were discovered in Russia in 1947 and published by the Moscow State Publishing House in 1948.

Boosey & Hawkes, as successors to the original publishers A. Gutheil (S. et N. Koussevitzky), first published this complete, re-engraved edition of Op. 33 in 1969, in completion of a project initiated over 70 years ago, and in fulfillment of the evident intentions of Gutheil, who originally advertised a complete edition but never issued it.

A very few minor editorial amendations and corrections of the Gutheil text have been included; the former are clearly indicated as such. The only pedaling marked by Rachmaninoff appears in the closing bars of Op. 33, No. 2. The fingerings, where given, also follow the original text.

Acknowledgement is made to Mr. Maurice Cole and Mr. Robert Threlfall for their valuable assistance in the preparation of this edition.

London, 1985

NOTE: For the 2006 reprint the opportunity has been taken to correct or amend some long-standing errors and omissions in Op. 33, which date from the original engravings (1914, 1948) and from the 1969 re-engraving.

Etudes-Tableaux, Op. 39

No. 2 is built almost entirely out of a syncopated falling two-note motif with a simple triplet accompaniment. The harmonic progressions are unpredictable, particularly in the central section, and this, combined with an almost total absence of the long melodic lines, creates an atmosphere of great loneliness.

No. 7 has a nightmare quality. The disjointed chorale-like opening is only briefly recalled at the end. The middle section consists of a lonely melody in the bass which is ultimately swamped by its accompaniment – an obsessive sixteenth-note figure which builds to a desperate climax before subsiding into silence.

No. 8 begins as if it might be a 'moderato' variation of the theme from No. 3, but much more music appears in the central sections before the opening rocking movement returns in conclusion.

— Peter Donohoe

Publisher's Note: Etudes-Tableaux, Op. 39

The original edition of *Etudes-Tableaux*, Op. 39 was published in separate numbers (RMV 333-341) by Edition Russe de Musique (Russischer-Musikverlag), Berlin, in 1920. As successors to S. et N. Koussevitzky, Boosey & Hawkes re-issued the separate numbers in 1950. The present edition is a further reprint, from the original, in one volume, making a companion to the new edition of *Etudes-Tableaux*, Op. 33 issued complete in 1969.

London, 1985

A MONSIEUR A. ARENSKY

MORCEAUX DE FANTAISIE
Elégie

SERGE RACHMANINOFF
Op. 3, No. 1

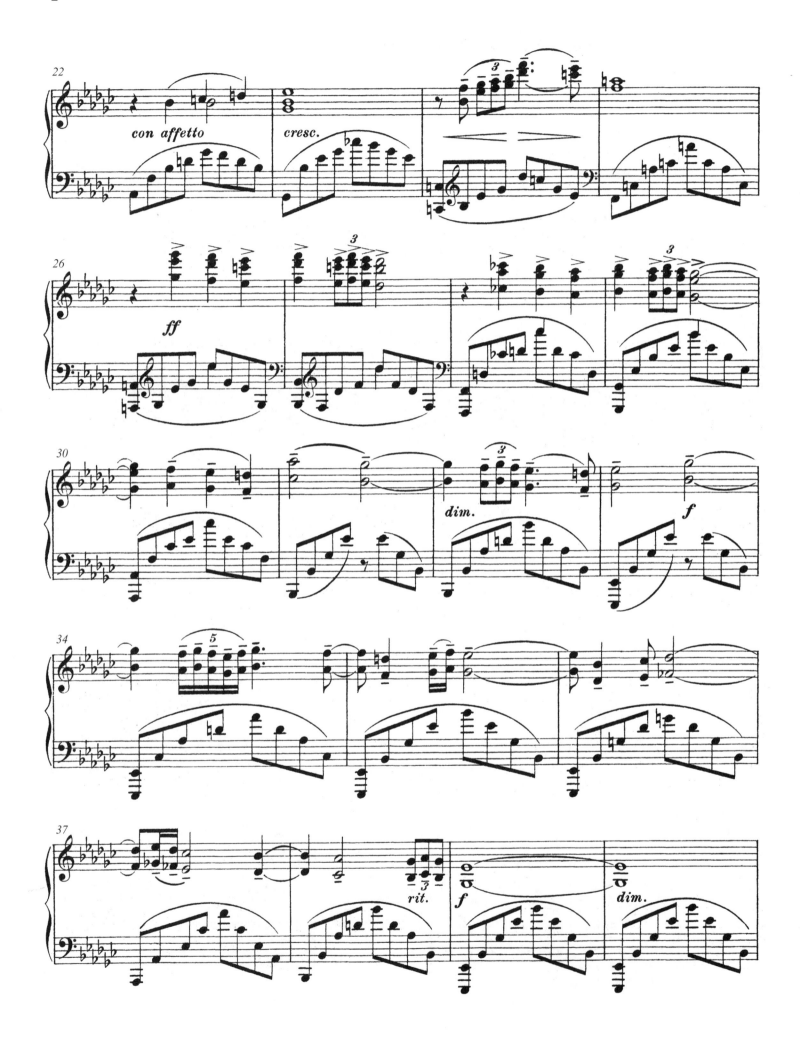

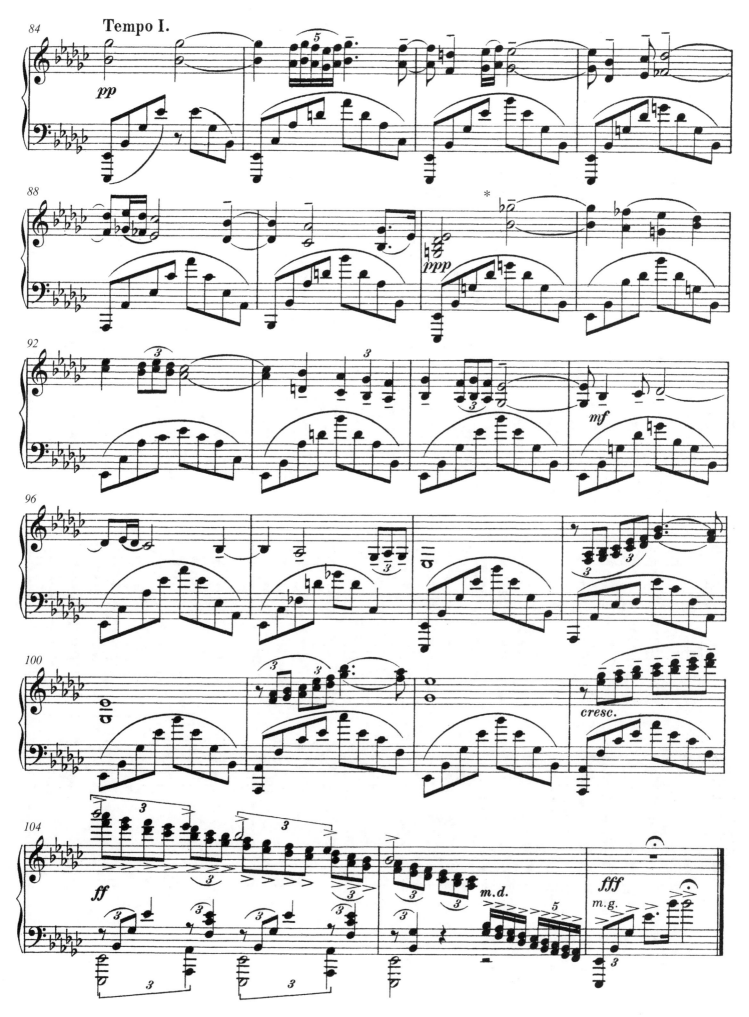

2

*This ♭ is in both MS and original edition

Prélude

SERGE RACHMANINOFF
Op. 3, No. 2

Mélodie

SERGE RACHMANINOFF
Op. 3, No. 3

Polichinelle

SERGE RACHMANINOFF
Op. 3, No. 4

Sérénade

SERGE RACHMANINOFF
Op. 3, No. 5

A MONSIEUR PAUL PABST

MORCEAUX DE SALON

SERGE RACHMANINOFF
Op. 10, No. 1

Nocturne

Valse

SERGE RACHMANINOFF
Op. 10, No. 2

Barcarolle

SERGE RACHMANINOFF
Op. 10, No. 3

Mélodie

SERGE RACHMANINOFF
Op. 10, No. 4

Humoresque

SERGE RACHMANINOFF
Op. 10, No. 5

Romance

SERGE RACHMANINOFF
Op. 10, No. 6

Mazurka

SERGE RACHMANINOFF
Op. 10, No. 7

102 Un poco meno mosso

This page intentionally left blank to facilitate page turns.

A MONSIEUR A. ZATAYEVITCH

MOMENTS MUSICAUX

SERGE RACHMANINOFF
Op. 16, No. 1

Tempo I.

MOMENTS MUSICAUX

SERGE RACHMANINOFF
Op. 16, No. 3

MOMENTS MUSICAUX

SERGE RACHMANINOFF
Op. 16, No. 5

LILACS

SERGE RACHMANINOFF
Op. 21, No. 5

A MONSIEUR A. SILOTI

PRELUDE

SERGE RACHMANINOFF
Op. 23, No. 4

A MONSIEUR A. SILOTI

PRELUDE

SERGE RACHMANINOFF
Op. 23, No. 5

Un poco meno mosso.

poco a poco accelerando e cresc. al Tempo I

PRELUDE

SERGE RACHMANINOFF
Op. 23, No. 6

A MONSIEUR A. SILOTI

PRELUDE

SERGE RACHMANINOFF
Op. 23, No. 10

PRELUDE

SERGE RACHMANINOFF
Op. 32, No. 7

PRELUDE

SERGE RACHMANINOFF
Op. 32, No. 10

PRELUDE

SERGE RACHMANINOFF
Op. 32, No. 11

Allegretto.

This page intentionally left blank to facilitate page turns.

ETUDES-TABLEAUX

SERGE RACHMANINOFF
Op. 33, No. 3*
(Op. Posth.)

* See Publisher's Note on page vii.

** This flat sign in brackets in earlier editions is not in the MS.

ETUDES-TABLEAUX

SERGE RACHMANINOFF
Op. 39, No. 2

ETUDES-TABLEAUX

SERGE RACHMANINOFF
Op. 39, No. 7

ETUDES-TABLEAUX

SERGE RACHMANINOFF
Op. 39, No. 8